NOT THE END,
BUT THE
Beginning

Dear Cearnett Family –
This is a sweet book
showing the most im-
portant decision of our
lifetime. Love to you,
Nancy Garver

NOT THE END,
BUT THE
Beginning

A Parable
on Destiny

Nancy M. Garver

XULON PRESS

Xulon Press
2301 Lucien Way #415
Maitland, FL 32751
407.339.4217

www.xulonpress.com

Paperback ISBN-13: 978-1-66281-429-7
Ebook ISBN-13: 978-1-66281-430-3

Acknowledgments

First of all, my many thanks to my sweet 14-year-old granddaughter, Cate Dahman, for her perspective from a teen's viewpoint in the writing of this book, as well as to her four sketches in regard to the development of the Monarch butterfly.

Next, the editing of Eileen Fitzgerald was very valuable to me, as she observed the story from beginning to end and gave me her very important appraisal, as she read of the progression of the magnificent plans of God in regard to each of two unlikely subjects and how they totally relate.

Last of all, I am grateful to my wonderful husband, Bob, for his technical knowledge, which is far above mine, and how he instructed me in the presentation to the Publisher, the finalization of this finished work.

TABLE OF CONTENTS

Isaiah 46:10

I DECLARE THE END FROM THE BEGINNING, AND FROM LONG AGO WHAT IS NOT YET DONE, SAYING: MY PLAN WILL TAKE PLACE AND I WILL DO ALL MY WILL.

Introduction
To a Miracle

I t's a lazy, sunny Fall afternoon. You can hear the sounds of dogs barking. Children's laughing can be heard as they swing back-and-forth on the swing set next door. There you are – sitting under a patio table umbrella with a tall glass of lemonade at your fingertips. This is just a typical Fall day with nothing unusual or out-of-the ordinary going on. Cars are driving past your house on their way to one destination after another. It's peaceful and relaxing.

All of a sudden a beautiful orange, black and white mosaic like a stained glass window with wings, flies past the patio and lands on a strongly scented purple blossom on your butterfly bush. What a sight. It has such delicate, fragile colors and intricate design on this brightly colored butterfly.

It drinks for a few minutes and then flies to other blooms, getting a fill up. It ends this drinking session by landing on one more flower and sips from this "fountain of nectar" as well. It takes off upward and flies out of sight.

Do you know that was not a random act of a particular butterfly? No sir!! This Monarch butterfly will be among millions of others of this particular fourth generation of their life cycle, that will be doing exactly the same thing in gardens and fields all over northern America every Fall. Three generations of Monarch butterflies before them will have been born and died in a very short span up to fifty days. But this fourth generation has a special assignment. They will drink, soar, and drink again until their flight takes them to the mountains of Central Mexico, a journey from Canada and upper United States to a destination of at least three thousand miles southwest. Hidden in this miraculous trip is a journey that has only been discovered in the past 45 years. It is a God-ordained and pre-programmed year after year, without fail.

Even more spectacular is the hidden meaning of this unbelievable journey. Portrayed in this generation of the Monarch butterfly's life cycle is the message of salvation, and how humans get to Heaven at life's end. Only through becoming a born-again believer in Jesus Christ can this happen. The example of the Monarch butterfly's fourth generation's long journey to Mexico demonstrates our trip to Heaven's door. As we gain access to that destination after we have breathed our last breath on earth, we will join millions of like-minded Christians who have successfully made that same trip. Believe me, we have not experienced the end of our lives, but rather, it's beginning.

Chapter 1

LAYING THE FOUNDATION

This is probably the most unique book you will ever read. Why? Because it is about two completely opposite subjects and yet how they have the same destiny. It's a parable. According to the World Book Dictionary – a parable is a story used to teach us some moral lesson or truth. **Proverbs 1:5-6 "Let a wise person listen and increase in learning, and let a discerning person obtain guidance – for understanding a proverb or a parable, the words of the wise, and their riddles."** In other words, a wise person increases in learning and obtains guidance through a parable. (1)

Such is the case in the New Testament portion of the Holy Bible. In this scripture Jesus Christ, the Son of God, used parables as symbols to effectively point out to those who did not know that He was sent from His Father, undeniable truths from nature that were simple stories easily understood, yet had great everlasting meaning.

One such example is found in the **Gospel of Matthew 13:24-30**. Here He presented another parable to them: **"The kingdom of Heaven may be compared to a man who sowed good seed in his field. But while people were sleeping his enemy came, sowed weeds among the wheat, and left. When the plants sprouted and produced grain, then the weeds also appeared. The landowner's servants came to him and said, 'Master, didn't you sow good seed in your field? Then where did the weeds come from?' "'An enemy did this,' "'So, do you want us to go and pull them up?' the servants asked Him. "'No,' He said. 'When you pull up the weeds, you might also uproot the wheat with them. Let both grow together until the harvest. At harvest time I'll tell the reapers: Gather the weeds first and tie them in bundles to burn them, but collect the wheat in My barn.'"**

The story begins with the Son of God planting good seed (believers) in his field (the earth) that will develop into full life spans of wheat. The believers and unbelievers, wheat and tares, grow side by side on earth. At a casual glance, one may not easily see the difference between the two. The slaves (angels) asked permission from Jesus to go and gather up the tares. God said **"No." "If that were done believers and unbelievers would both be harmed."** His solution: **"Let them grow together through each generation until the harvest** (the end of time)." The reapers (angels) would then gather the tares (unbelievers) and throw them into the fire (Hell). The wheat (believers) would be gathered into God's barn (which is Heaven).

This simple story about believers and unbelievers demonstrates that there are two very distinct eternal destinies for all of humanity. Heaven's provision has been made. But we, as humans, have to make a choice. Do we want to be a stalk of wheat, or a counterfeit weed that grows in the grain fields alongside the wheat?

It's totally our decision, not God's. **He can't – and won't – choose for us.**

A vivid illustration from nature will distinctively prove that through the four life cycles of the regal Monarch butterfly, they very accurately prove the following truths from the Bible without a shadow of a doubt:

All humans are born spiritually without God at birth. **Romans 3:23** says: **"For all have sinned and fall short of the glory of God." John 1:12-13 says: "But to all who did receive Him, He gave them the right to be children of God, to those who believe in His name, who were born, not of natural descent, or of the will of the flesh, or the will of man, but of God."**

All human beings are God's creation, but **only** those "born into His family" by adoption, can call Him Father. Babies that pass away go to Heaven, but those who know the difference between good and evil, will have to make a choice as to whether or not they will listen to what God declares in the Bible.

What happens spiritually to that person at the "new birth"? **John 3:3 – Jesus replied, "Truly I tell you, unless someone is born again, he cannot see the kingdom of God."** Jesus is not speaking of a natural birth, but a supernatural one that comes from His Spirit. This comes only when we reach out and confess our sins and accept the gift of God through His Son who agreed to take on the sins of every human being on the face of this earth – that has ever lived or ever will live. We couldn't pay the price ourselves. It was much too costly.

In order to become a "new creature in Christ", there must be these steps:

As Romans 3:23 says that every human being on this earth has sinned, and we accept Jesus as our personal Savior, we give Him all our sins so He can wipe them away as though they never happened. **II Corinthians 5:17** declares: **"Therefore, if anyone is in Christ, he is a new creation; the old has passed away, and see, the new has come."** Jesus, the Son of God, who never sinned once, took all the sins of every human being that has ever or will live on this earth. We reach out and accept that fact. Jesus said in **John 14:6: "I Am the way, the truth, and the life. No one comes to the Father except through Me." There are NOT many ways to Heaven – ONLY ONE WAY – through God's Son, Jesus Christ.**

By making the decision to reach out to Jesus and ask Him to forgive us of our sins and come into our life, He will forgive us and help us live a meaningful life.

This transformation in us will cause our spirit (which contacts God), our soul (which is our will, intellect, mind, personality and emotions) to literally "fly away" to who have gone before us, other believers who knew Jesus as personal Savior in their lifetime, and Old Testament saints. **I Thessalonians 4:16-17 "For the Lord Himself will descend from heaven with a shout, with the archangel's voice, and with the trumpet of God, and the dead in Christ will rise first. Then we who are still alive, who are left, will be caught up together with them in the clouds to meet the Lord in the air, and so we will always be with the Lord."**

I am excited to explain a very similar process which you will definitely see illustrated in the life of the fascinating insect called the Monarch butterfly, also known as the milkweed butterfly. It was first discovered in Australia way back in 1874 by Samuel H. Scutter and was originally named The Wanderer. (2)

WHAT IN THE WORLD DOES A MONARCH BUTTERFLY AND A HUMAN HAVE IN COMMON? EVERYTHING:

EVEN THOUGH ONE IS AN INSECT AND THE OTHER A HUMAN BEING.

And now, I am delighted to take you on an awesome adventure. It involves two unlikely characters. But you will be able to connect them both at the end of the book. Hang on, as these two take their astounding trip **HOME**.

Chapter 2

CIRCULAR BEGINNINGS

This exquisite creature's fourth generation in North America begins its existence in Canada and the upper regions of the United States. But before it has reached HOME (or its place of destiny) where they will always complete its life cycle in the mountains of central Mexico along with millions of other Monarch butterflies from various parts of the United States east of the Rocky Mountains, four generations will have lived. This potential hibernating Monarch butterfly will travel alone most of the way and with others the rest of the way, as it continues on its long and very difficult journey across the land mass of the United States - with one destination in mind: get HOME to Mexico **by a certain date** in order to be included in that generation of butterflies that will insure the next generation coming after it. (1)

How does this lovely regal butterfly know when to leave Canada or the upper regions of the United States and when it is to arrive in another country 3000 miles away? How does this fragile insect endure all kinds of conditions to fulfill its God-ordained responsibility to its species? It will fly. You heard me right. **IT MUST FLY THERE.** It will make it if it can and doesn't encounter the obstacles that it will definitely come up against on this once-in-a-lifetime journey. Many will never arrive in Mexico. But fortunately, millions WILL arrive there safely – in order for God to keep this beautiful insect surviving generation after generation.

Only this fourth generation of the Monarch butterfly gets to its true destination through life and death cycles. The other generations live only two to seven weeks, but have laid eggs producing caterpillars which turn into adult butterflies so their species will be assured of continuing on.

Each time an egg is laid, a larva emerges and grows into a caterpillar. A female can lay up to 250 eggs a day, and, believe it or not, one female

Monarch butterfly in captivity laid 1179 eggs in one 24 hour period. Each egg weighs only 0.50 milligrams.

A single female Monarch that has its beginnings in North America becomes fertile and can deposit from 300-500 eggs in a lifetime -- eggs that are the size of the head of a pin. Each elongated egg is laid separately on the underside of the leaves of the milkweed plant with quick drying "glue", in order to hide it from the view of any predator, so that the small caterpillar is able to develop. One plant is capable of having countless eggs on many leaves. How does the female Monarch butterfly do that? (2)

A serious problem for the Monarch butterfly in North America is the black swallowort plant. Monarch butterflies may lay their eggs on these plants since they produce stimuli very similar to the milkweed plant. But once the eggs hatch, the small caterpillars are poisoned by the deadly ingredients within its leaves.

After the eggs are successfully laid, the parents die. Their mission is now complete. Each egg, in the shape of a cone, is very tiny and creamy white, and will turn pale yellow, and develops a circular black head. Its weight is 0.46 grams, will be only 1.2" long, emerging in just 3-5 days.

Similarly, a human being also begins its life through the process of a man and a woman joining together – and the egg in the mother's body that is no longer than a period at the end of this sentence starts on its life's journey. The baby begins to live and in about 42 weeks he/she is born, weighing an average of 6 pounds. (3)

After the butterfly larva chews its way out of the egg, it turns around and eats its eggshell, upon which it depended. It is simply doing what it is programmed to do, in order to give itself nourishment until it can begin eating milkweed leaves. The small larva has totally separated itself from where it originated.

We, too, have to lay down our past so it will not hold us back from becoming all God wants us to be.

Philippians 3:13b-14, says: **" but one thing I do: forgetting what lies behind and reaching forward to what is ahead, I pursue as my goal the prize promised by God's heavenly call in Christ Jesus."**

Just as the small larva has totally eliminated from where it originated, we also have to lay down our past that will not only hinder us but hold us back from becoming all God the Father has created us to be.

The Lord has a definite plan, which is a perfect destiny for each and every one of us. Each life has a definite purpose and plan originating from the mind of God.

Jeremiah 29:11-13 "For I know the plans I have for you" - this is the Lord's declaration - "plans for your wellbeing, not for disaster, to give you a future an a hope. You will call to me and come and pray to me, and I will listen to you. You will seek me and find me when you search for me with all your heart. I will be found by you." How comforting to know that God knows us all individually and has a wonderful life planned for us if we live in obedience to Him. When there is a day-to-day relationship with God, we will grow to know exactly what that plan is for our life.

Chapter 3

CHOMP, CHOMP, DUMP, DUMP

Monarch caterpillars are eating machines munching only the leaves beginning at the edges of the leaves plus the flowers of the milkweed plant. One milkweed plant can be host to a number of caterpillars at the same time. There exists inside of each leaf a rubber-type substance resembling an oozing latex that saturates those leaves on the inside. The larva do nothing but chomp, chomp, dump, dump. From egg to adult butterfly, it will have grown 2700 times its original weight, and the male or female Monarch butterfly produces frass (which it eliminates) as a result of so much eating. (1)

On the first day of its existence it consumes its weight in food. It must do this because it's on a definite time line of existence. The milkweed is about the only plant the Monarch butterfly larva is able to eat. Through this milky-white substance it gets what it needs to enable it to store fat and nutrients to carry it through this pupa or larva stage for two weeks. About the only variation in their food source are 100 plus varieties of milkweed in existence in this country.

As sure as there are many species of milkweed which is the caterpillar's main diet, we too, in America, will never be able to say we never had access to spiritual food called the Bible in its many forms such as CD's, DVD's, iPads, smart phones, tablets, etc. to download the Bible onto them. There are TV and radio programs, computer access, books and ebooks. These are all geared to lead, instruct and guide the population of this country as each individual sincerely investigates how to live here on earth as God would direct, with definite guidelines to reach our eternal home in heaven. But God in His infinite wisdom gave us a will to accept or reject these explicit instructions and the way to live a godly life here and then how to reach that glorious eternal destination at life's end. **We are not marionettes who dance before God or cower in fear of Him. He urges us to choose, not reject Him and His perfect plan for our life.** Humans are rebels in their spirit by nature but if we just inch our way toward Him, He will run full speed ahead toward us.

John 4:24 "God is spirit, and those who worship Him must worship Him in spirit and in truth."

Chapter 4

ALWAYS BEING WATCHED

The Monarch larva grows day by day, increasing in size dramatically. **Inside the leaves of the milkweed are all the nutrients needed to transform this caterpillar into a beautiful adult butterfly.** As it grows it takes on black, white and yellow stripes around its circumference that resemble strip farming (a farmer's field where he plants his crops in alternating rows, one after the other in a definite pattern). It's hard to believe, but the fat gotten from the milkweeds will carry the fourth generation to Mexico. There they hibernate on trees by the millions.

On the image below, you will plainly see the first caterpillar size as compared to the last size. All of this comes to pass in two short weeks!

These colors on the caterpillar are definitely used to keep its predators at arms' length by proclaiming loud and clear, "I'm poisonous." For some reason birds are programmed to be able to recognize that the caterpillar's bold colors are relaying to them that they are off limits to eat. And through the black, yellow and white stripes they declare: "Don't even try to eat me or I will make you vomit."

This fatty substance inside the leaves can even cause havoc to a human, should they ingest it!

Its size increases notably by the day. Its "skin" – or instar -- is really an outer covering that must be shed four times – or instars - as it grows too big for this tight skin. When the final shedding occurs the old skin drops in a heap in an unrecognizable black mass below, as it is perched up above as it prepares for its transformation.

During our human existence the devil tries to kill us as well, any chance he gets! He has a passion to see to it that we reject God who created us and wants a relationship with us in our day to day living and who also wants us to spend eternity with Him in Heaven. Or... if the enemy miserably fails to end our life he will do everything within his power to entice us to withdraw from God while causing us to willfully walk away from the One who has lovingly, willingly allowed His Son Jesus to pay the price for the forgiveness of our sins through His sacrifice. **John 14:6** states: **Jesus told him, "I am The Way, The Truth, and The life. No one comes to the Father except through Me."**

Chapter 5

MANY BLACK SHOES

The Monarch butterfly caterpillar grows to 2" long and is fully grown in only 9- 14 days. **Protruding from its sides are five pairs of legs with what looks exactly like little patent leather shoes, four with spats and one pair in back without them, in order for it to have a strong grip as it travels throughout the milkweed plant leaf after leaf.**

There are three pairs of "real legs" which are called thoracic legs, with claws attached. The five pairs behind these, which are called anal prologs extend in a backward direction. All of these will totally disappear after the pupa or caterpillar stage is complete. In addition to that, there are two pairs of sensory tentacles; one long pair on the head and a shorter pair on the end of the abdomen. From a distance it's difficult to tell whether the caterpillar is coming or going. (1)

And isn't that what we humans experience at times? Life can get so hectic, filled with things to do and places to go. We get frustrated, full of stress and sometimes become overwhelmed because we haven't stayed close to the Lord and enjoyed His presence. Night comes and we flop into bed totally spent, not knowing whether we are coming or going as well. We wanted to fellowship with God and read His Word, but "life" got in the way.

We also will wear many "pairs of shoes" as well from our baby shoes to those of an adult walking our path of life. We go here and there; some of us may travel long distances, even to the ends of the earth. For others, they may never travel far from their city of birth. But you know it really doesn't matter how far we roam from our entrance into this earth. It's what we get done for the Lord – from a bed or wheelchair, on foot, by car, boat, plane or ship – wherever we are, in whatever shape we are in. We are all equally important to God. He has no favorites.

From these eight pairs of legs on the caterpillar, the first three pairs will become another type of legs altogether in appearance and function which will be totally capable of walking, but yet be light enough to enable itself to become airborne without effort when it becomes a Monarch butterfly. This larva that becomes a caterpillar will shed or molt its instars four times during this stage. A new and larger instar will cover its body each time. When this happens the caterpillar will outgrow its "outer man". (2)

As humans, the "real us" dwells inside our bodies which in reality is a space suit made perfect for our existence on this earth, where we live out our lifetime. The Apostle Paul refers to this in **II Corinthians 12:2 "I know a man in Christ who was caught up to the third heaven fourteen years ago. Whether he was in the body or out of the body, I don't know: God knows. 3: I know that this man - whether in the body or out of body I don't know; God knows-4: was caught up into paradise and heard inexpressible words, which a human being is not allowed to speak."** Each believer is told to walk in the spirit (which is the real us) and not in the flesh (which is our outer man), as **Romans 8:5** says: **"For those who live according to the flesh have their minds set on the things of the flesh, but those who live according to the Spirit have their minds set on things of the Spirit."**

In other words, we can be ruled by what we see, think, do, or say, OR we can be guided by what our spirit deep inside us is telling us as to how to act and react according to what God tells us. When we do what He wants, He is pleased. If we do the opposite, we get ourselves into deep trouble

Because we are a three part being: spirit, soul and body, we are fully capable of walking in the spirit realm day after day. To walk in the realm of the flesh (always wanting and doing our own desires, through our will) – we do not please God. He desires that we walk being led by the Holy Spirit, even though doing what we don't want to and going where we would rather not. In these hard places in life, God is by our side, causing those things to work out for us so He is made known to those around us. **Romans 8:28** says: **"We know that all things work together for the good of those who love God, who are called according to His purpose."**

Chapter 6

THE SACRIFICE OF LAMBS

In the Book of Genesis **Chapter 2:7-3:24**, there is a story of humankind's first parents, Adam and Eve. Because it is such a long passage of scripture, I strongly advise you to read it carefully. In **2:8-9** it says: **"The Lord God planted a garden in Eden, in the east, and there He placed the man He had formed. The Lord God caused to grow out of the ground every tree pleasing in appearance and good for food, including the tree of life in the middle of the garden, as well as the tree of knowledge of good and evil." Verses 16-17: "And the Lord God commanded THE MAN, "You are free to eat from any tree of the garden, but you must not eat from the tree of knowledge** of good and evil, for on that day you eat from it, you will certainly die."

Verse :18 Then the Lord God said: "It's not good for man to be alone. I will make a helper corresponding to him." So that's what He did. He made Eve from Adam's body and she became his wife. These two people were sinless, and talked to God daily...such tranquility, peace and joy that must have been!

But one day the devil appeared in the garden and surprised Eve with a temptation to disobey what God had told them. She and her husband had never had one temptation to do anything wrong before, and they had enjoyed constant conversations with the Lord without any interruptions.

At that moment, Eve didn't think it through. Instead, she impulsively gave in to the devil's temptation. She knew of the explicit instructions given to Adam about the two trees in the garden; one they could eat from, the other they were forbidden, lest they die. She told the devil that she and Adam were not allowed to eat from **OR** touch the tree of the knowledge of good and evil.

In the devil's temptation he spoke words that caused Eve to doubt what God had said. In

Chapter 3:4 it says **"No! You will not die. :5 In fact God knows that when you eat it your eyes will be opened and you will be like God, knowing knowing good and evil."** Be like God Himself? What a wonderful possibility that seemed to be, as she listened intently.

Eve gave in to the temptation, and plucked a piece of fruit and ate it. What's really amazing is that God had given those instructions to Adam, not Eve. Adam knew what God had told him. And yet, he also submitted to the temptation to disobey God. It says in **verse 6: "Adam was with her and he ate the piece of fruit."** What happened as a result of that disobedience? **Verse 7: "Then the eyes of both of them were opened, and they knew they were naked; so they sewed fig leaves together and made coverings for themselves."** That disobedient act was their attempt to cover their sin with their own works!

To say that God was angry is an understatement! They had willfully sinned and disobeyed His perfect will for them. **He had to punish their disobedience.**

But in His mercy, He made a way out for them. **Chapter 3:21** tells us how the Lord stepped in.

"The Lord God made clothing from animal skins for this man and his wife, and He clothed them."

He had to kill an innocent lamb. It had to give its life to cover the willful sins of Adam and Eve, the only two people on this earth. But God also had to drive them out of Eden. No more would they have everything given to them by the Lord. By the sweat of their brow they would have to provide for their own survival. **Their attempts to be innocent before God again would be impossible, apart from God.**

This one act of judgment from God upon two sinners – is the groundwork for what would be required in the future for all sinners from that day forward. In the Old Testament, a guarantee of those living during that time was the fact that innocent lambs had to shed their blood as an act of substitution on the Day of Atonement, which is a Jewish Holy Day which comes between September and October, when the Jewish people were commanded to ask God to forgive them of their many sins of the past year, through the High Priest who would intervene in their behalf.

In the New Testament we have the story of the birth of the Son of God, born to die for the sins of all human beings. He came for the sole purpose of dying in our place on the cross. So when we, in faith, reach out and accept His sacrifice for us, and proclaim it from our lips that **He has become our substitute and has paved the way for us to go HOME to Heaven,** then we have that assurance. **Romans 10:9-10 "If you confess with your mouth, 'Jesus is Lord', and believe it in your heart that God raised Him from the dead, you will be saved. One believes with the heart, resulting in righteousness, and one confesses with the the mouth, resulting in salvation."**

If we do that, we are assured of Heaven. We can't get there any other way except through Jesus Christ. Everything we have thought, said, or done that is outside of God's will, **will be forgiven and forgotten as if they never happened in the first place.** All because of the sacrifice of Jesus, the Lamb of God, as John the Baptist called Him in **John 1:29**, and His willingness to take our punishment as our substitute before God, His Father.

Chapter 7

IT'S A TRANSFORMATION

Returning to the caterpillar: When it reaches 2" long it becomes very restless so it looks for a place to pupate (or the stage needed to transform it from one type of creature to another). It marches off this plant that it has been consuming one leaf at a time with all five pairs of legs moving in tandem and will begin to construct its chrysalis which will be somewhere else such as a secluded branch. The chrysalis is a small light green waxy bag that will totally encase the caterpillar while it is changing from a caterpillar to a beautiful Monarch butterfly. (1)

The caterpillar attaches its spinneret (hind end) to

a branch with a silk-like pad inserting the small hooks located in the anal prolog legs (or rear end caboose). Very very slowly it releases itself from the attached end - while fully trusting that it will not fall. **It is now upside down and will remain turned up slightly in the form of a J for no more than twenty-four hours. At that point it will dramatically change once again.** During this suspended period of time, it hangs between Heaven and earth, so to speak.

Just as the caterpillar is hanging with no way of escape, it serves as a type of Jesus Who hung suspended on the cross, taking the full punishment for all the sins of humankind, as well as all our sicknesses. **ISAIAH 53:4-5 "YET HE HIMSELF BORE OUR SICKNESSES, AND HE CARRIED OUR PAINS; BUT WE IN TURN REGARDED HIM STRICKEN, STRUCK DOWN BY GOD, AND AFFLICTED. BUT HE WAS PIERCED BECAUSE OF OUR REBELLION, CRUSHED BECAUSE OF OUR INIQUITIES; PUNISHMENT FOR OUR PEACE WAS ON HIM AND WE ARE HEALED BY HIS WOUNDS."**

This scripture was written by the Prophet Isaiah 750 years before the death of Jesus. Crucifixion **was not** a form of punishment by death in the days of Isaiah, yet God revealed this to him so he could record it, proving God knows all things.

What Jesus did is a fact. The Son of God willingly gave His life for you and me. He took our place of punishment for all of us for sins He never committed **because He was sinless**.

Chapter 8

HANG ON TIGHT

I n Matthew 27:50-51 it says: **"But Jesus cried out again with a loud voice and gave up His spirit. Suddenly, the curtain of the sanctuary was torn in two from the top to bottom, the earth quaked, and the rocks were split."**

This veil had separated God from the High Priest (who himself is separated from the common people). God dwelled in the temple in the Holy Place, which was only accessible to the High Priest. Once the ripping began there was no turning back. It would be a permanent statement from Almighty God that now says that all people on this earth, no matter who they are or where they dwell, have the privilege and opportunity to come into His presence at any moment without a High Priest as a mediator as the Old Testament describes it. But now, since God Himself ripped the veil from top to bottom, this signifies it was a once-and-for all act, showing He would forever give all people access to Him 24 hours of every day. We are now without excuse. God is waiting for each of us to freely come to Him.

After 24 hours in this hanging upside down position the Monarch caterpillar begins to shake. In this process it gyrates, twists, pumps and pulsates as it is being reshaped. It looks like it doesn't want to submit – but it must. Resignation is complete. **That which was the original form of caterpillar will NEVER be seen again.** The movement has totally stopped. This process could take up to an hour to complete. The old skin has split from bottom to top and it turns into a black mass of unrecognizable substance that just drops away. This includes its head, feelers, little black feet and even its eyes. (**God has completed His work and has shut the door to it ever returning to what it once was.**) It has disappeared into a small pale green chrysalis with a specific shape unlike what it originally looked like. The caterpillar has been reduced to l/4 of its original size. What is seen is actually the caterpillar exposed.

According to the late Dr. Lincoln Brower: "What happens inside the chrysalis is phenomenal. In this changing of form, a biological miracle takes place inside. All of the tissue of the caterpillar is being totally changed into something described as a rich culture medium. Several sets of little cells that relate to different parts of the body are called "imaginal disks". In reality they are like little groups of embryonic cells that start to grow very quickly. One of these imaginal disks is transformed into a wing, a leg, etc., making up the entire Monarch body. **During the first 3-4 days there now appears a bag of rich fluid media that the cells of the butterfly are growing on. This is truly a miraculous biological process of transformation within the small chrysalis. The entire internal contents of the caterpillar are totally transformed.** During this process of transition from caterpillar to butterfly it loses half its weight. This proves that this process of metamorphosis (changing its form or substance) consumes enormous amounts of energy in order to do this transformation. All of its waste products are unable to be disposed of so they accumulate inside. After the butterfly emerges this accumulation drops from the butterfly in a reddish colored liquid." (Having seen this happen myself, that reddish colored liquid looks just like shed blood.)

Research Professor Lincoln P. Brower had been at Sweet Briar College beginning in July 1997 and was an admirer of Monarch butterflies for more than 50 years.

His profound statement concerning this insect: "Why should we care about the Monarch? For the same reason we care about the Mona Lisa or the beauty of Mozart's music." This zoologist and biologist had studied the overwintering migration and conservation biology of the Monarch butterfly, and he was confident that these butterflies undergo the most extra-ordinary annual migration on this earth. He passed away in 2002. (1) (2)

Chapter 9

GOD'S GLORY DOTS

After shedding its old skin, the newly exposed skin is soft and will dry clear. Its temporary quarters are the beautifully designed light jade green exoskeleton – which will serve as a protective covering over the developing butterfly inside. The clear covering has a very recognizable gold line around its circumference close to the top where it is attached to a branch. Also appearing are evenly spaced gold dots that have appeared all around the bottom of the clear casing. It would seem as if God's glory stamp of approval is now on it. It doesn't sparkle until after the first 24 hours of the formation of the chrysalis. (1) **The Greek name for chrysalis is "golden crown" which was the Greek**

sign of royalty. This crown of golden points is the diadem on it. The caterpillar that once existed is no more and this "rich culture medium" will do its work on the inside while on the outside it remains still. No more movement will be seen when looking at the outside until the day it comes forth as an adult Monarch butterfly. The process inside will change this creature that chewed every moment to one that will only drink nectar; from one that only walked and was earthbound, to one that will walk when necessary but fly predominantly and is now Heaven bound.

A human being also will go from an impregnated egg (which takes about 24 hours) – being the same time for the mating of the male and female Monarch butterfly, to a fetus only 1/2" long up and grow to an average of 18.5" long and weighing around six pounds in 38-42 weeks, hidden from view (except for the ultrasound). **Psalm 139:13-16 "For it was You who created MY inward parts; You knit ME together in MY mother's womb. I will praise You because I have**

Egg

been remarkably and wondrously made. Your works are wondrous and I know this very well. MY bones were not hidden from You when I was made in secret, when I was formed in the depths of the earth. Your eyes saw ME when I was form-less, all MY days were written in Your book and planned before a single one of them began." Do you see how much love God has for each one of who has ever been born? We are all unique, and we are born with a **specific purpose.** (Did you also notice that we were a person before we came out from our mother's womb?) (2)

In addition, what happens to humankind also cannot be seen either during the transforma-tion process of becoming born again, or that of becoming conformed into an adopted child of God **from** a child of the devil. As Jesus was speaking to His countrymen, the Jews, they questioned Him as recorded in **John 8:42-45: "If God were your Father, you would love Me, because I came from God and I am He."**

For I didn't come of My own, but He sent Me. Why don't you understand what I say"? Because you cannot listen to My word. You are of your father the devil, and you want to carry out

your father's desires. **He was a murderer from the beginning and does not stand in the truth, because there is no truth in him. When he tells a lie, he speaks from his own nature, because he is a liar and the father of lies."**

A person must see their need for Jesus and must accept His finished work at the cross. We must fully recognize He is the Son of God Who died and went to hell, taking all our punishment. According to **Romans 5:10** it says: **"For if while we were enemies we were reconciled to God through the death of His Son, much more, having been reconciled, we shall be saved by His life."** He went to hell when He did nothing to merit that trip. But fortunately He couldn't be held there because He was without sin. We accept His sacrifice and we believe that this act was a once-and-for-all action. Salvation is an absolutely free gift that has nothing whatsoever to do with the doing of our good works in order to attain it. We have to become God's child. **II Corinthians 5:21** states clearly: **"He made the One Who did not know sin to be sin for us, so that in Him we might become the righteousness of God."**

What a humbling fact from God's Word. In other words, what we were and did before our accepting Jesus into our lives – was put on Jesus at the cross so we don't have to carry it anymore. He guarantees that this will cause a dramatic change for the rest of our life – as we determine in our heart to follow and obey Him. By repeating the following prayer out loud, you too can become a member of God's royal family:

Chapter 10

THE SINNER'S PRAYER

Dear God, I acknowledge that I have thought, done and said things in my life that have hurt You. I have held things inside that I should have let go; some of them for a long time. I acknowledge that I am a sinner who needs You to forgive me. I come to You, asking for Your forgiveness. Take all thoughts, words, and actions away from me that make You sad. I recognize that Jesus took my place of punishment and I ask Him to come into my life and change me into what He wants me to be. Thank You that You have a wonderful plan for my life, and that Heaven is my future HOME because of what Jesus has done for me. I now receive that forgiveness for my sins, never to be remembered by You again. In Jesus' name. Amen.

When we "die to self" (wanting to do what **we** insist on doing, whether it's right in God's eyes or not), our old nature which caused us to sin, does not have a hold on us anymore. Our desire to always do something wrong has stopped controlling us. Oh yes, we will still sin again, but if we ask the Lord to forgive us, He will. We will want to please Him and follow what is written in the Bible for our day-to-day living.

When we do that, we are back on "speaking terms" with the Lord.

If you have a "slip up", pray **I John 1:9** from your heart: **"If we confess our sins, He is faithful and righteous to forgive us our sins and to cleanse us from all unrighteousness."** What assurance.

To grow in your new-found faith, I suggest that you contact online:

Billy Graham Evangelistic Association - Grow Your Faith

They have available to you, many resources to help increase your faith in Jesus Christ.

I also suggest you find a Bible believing church where you can attend and become involved with the work of the Lord there.

Chapter 11

A Miracle Happens

T he chrysalis, which is the exposed skin of the caterpillar that has hardened, remains green for about ten days to two weeks. **Then, all of a sudden it turns jet black.** What we are looking at is the clear covering around the black butterfly wings, which are curled around and around in a tubular fashion on the inside of the chrysalis. It gives the image of a piece of jade jewelry. The butterfly that was green the day before will now come forth as a beautiful and majestic orange, black, and white Monarch butterfly.

"I caught a Monarch butterfly! To me, Your Majesty!" - City Folknookipedia.com wiki/ Monarch-butterfly (1)

This same transformation applies to humans as God's holiness envelops us and changes each of us into a new person – transforming us into an adopted child of God. **Ephesians 1:5 "He predestined us to be adopted as sons (and daughters) through Jesus Christ for Himself, according to the good pleasure of His will."**

The chrysalis has turned a smoky color and becomes brittle and then splits from the bottom to the top. The golden band has turned black, and the gold dots have become dull. It looks like the chrysalis – as well as what's inside – have been charred and it now resembles stiff cellophane wrap. **It has been through the "fire" of transformation.**

Jesus Christ became that same type of offering for the whole human race. He took our place in Hell where we should be going, but instead promises us Heaven and all of its beauty in eternity with Him.

The day of the miracle has finally arrived. The mature butterfly emerges from its burial clothes, so to speak, after this short 10-14 day stay, in which very rapid changes have taken place. The Monarch butterfly has been transformed from death to life and **has been "resurrected"**, so to speak.

The butterfly carefully wiggles out and drops upside down, like it was when it entered the chrysalis as a caterpillar. However, it immediately turns right side up, still clinging tightly to the split chrysalis for support. Its wings are small and crumpled looking. Hemolymph, which is a blood-like substance is pumped into those crumpled wings until they are full and strong enough to fly, which takes up to half an hour. What a treat for the eyes!

The newly emerged Monarch butterfly will remain suspended in that position motionless for a couple of hours until its wings dry thoroughly so it can fly and soar. During this waiting period, a puddle of liquid drops from it, which is the accumulated waste that occurred during metamorphosis.

The Monarch butterfly is relatively small and from wingtip to wingtip it measures about three inches. It has a body almost 1" long. There are four wings that are a field of yellow, orange or gold, and there are veins of black running throughout.

Thickest in front is a band of black that winds around the wings. Its body is also black in color. This band is speckled with white spots that are larger in front but smaller in back.

The eight pairs of stubby legs used for walking when it was a caterpillar have now been transposed into three pairs of long jointed legs with two "fingers" at the end of each. The two front legs will remain close to the body and are not used. Now it will only use the middle and hind legs.

On the black head of the Monarch butterflies is a pair of antennae, compound eyes, and a split tongue that is "zipped together". It's thorax or chest contain muscles that make the legs and wings move.

A trademark of the Monarch is its exceptionally strong wings. The colorful bright sheen on their wings is actually a multitude of smooth protein polymer plates, called chitin. Each plate is measured in micrometers and is lined with a set of parallel grooves. The grooves also reduce drag, helping water and air to flow off their wings. Imagine this picture: the Monarch butterfly's body is constructed of thousands of intricate narrow "petals" with two points facing downward, lined up side by side, one layer overlapping the other, as if going down a roof. **The black veins in the wings are surrounded by thousands of colorful overlapping scales resembling roof shingles or fish scales. These powdery scales give the Monarch its beautiful majestic orange and black hue pattern.** (2)

Finally, the Monarch butterfly's abdomen has reduced itself to a normal size and **spreads its fully developed wings as "kingly robes" stretched outward.** It quivers to make sure it is ready to fly, and up it goes into the air – even though it has never flown before in its existence. It flies away to feed on flowers with its newly constructed straw-like flexible tongue called the proboscis. This uncoils so it can sip nectar, and recoils back up again into a spiral when not in use. It will then be on a search for nectar-producing flowers.

Now this beautiful Monarch butterfly has a reorganized body with no resemblance of its slow-moving caterpillar life but rather, its life will now be predominately filled with flying, not walking.

Chapter 12

ONE, TWO, THREE, FOUR

We have just completed one cycle of one Monarch butterfly. The four generations are actually different butterflies going through these four distinct stages in one year until it is time to start all over again with stage one and generation one.

These generations begin in February or March when fertilized eggs are deposited on milkweed plants in southern United States (and particularly Texas) after wintering in Mexico. Their trip north begins. (1)

In May or June the second generation is born as they travel northeast to Canada through North America.

The third generation is born from July to August as they continue to their designated path to Canada.

The last generation born in Canada and upper U.S. will be born and begin an adventure that in the natural is impossible to complete, but in the supernatural God will cause it to come to pass.

In the long and dangerous migration that lies ahead in September or October this fourth Monarch generation has something in their makeup called juvenile hormone or diapause, which prevents them from reproducing. This gives them increased longevity, as they have turned around and will head southwest to Mexico.

The western population of the Monarch flies to the central coastal area of southern California, particularly Pacific Grove and Santa Cruz where they will hibernate in the eucalyptus trees. (2)

All the rest will wind up 3000 miles southwest in central Mexico, in the same forests of oyamel fir trees in which their ancestors hibernated generation after generation. **Monarchs are the only insect that participates in this migration to warmer climates. This is the longest insect migration on earth.** There are two miraculous occurrences here. They have just come forth as a butterfly, never having flown before, will fly over a huge body of water, an extremely long trip over land, mountains and desert. They are on their way to a place they have never been but where they will meet together with other Monarchs by the millions. MIRACULOUS. Their migration is because of two reasons: 1. They can't withstand the cold temperatures and 2. Larvae food, which is milkweed plants, has lost their leaves in the winter in the north.

By the end of October the Monarch population east of the Rockies goes to Marijsosa Biosphere Reserve within the Trans-Mexican Volcanic Belt pine oak forests in the western central part of the Mexican states of Michoacan and Angangueo in Mexico. (3)

Small areas of the Monarch Butterfly Biosphere Reserve covering 200 square miles will be the destination of these butterflies. The tops of the trees high in the mountains of the reserve will become orange because of the numbers that have landed there to hibernate all winter. El Rosario sanctuary which is 10,000 feet above sea level and open to the public, is the largest visited area with thousands of visitors a day during this hibernation period. The Monarchs will spread themselves over the 500 ever-green and oak trees 100 feet above the forest floor that can only be reached by a steep climb up a hill surrounding the trees.

This fourth generation has begun its 3000-mile journey southwest from Canada to Mexico. They are shaped like a stealth airplane ("secret action" according to The World Book Dictionary) because they are really on a divinely orchestrated trip. We must realize that these newly hatched butterflies have never taken this carefully timed trip before and they haven't a clue as to how to get to their destination or where they are going. Miraculously these Monarchs will all get there every year to Mexico from different points of North America east of the Rocky mountains, just as their ancestors did for many many years before them. It is abso-lutely essential that these Monarchs use prevailing winds to get them to Mexico each year on time. From October to March there will be close to 50 million Monarchs who arrive at their destination, depending upon winds, their food supply, how many predators get them and their overall stamina.

Each Monarch will fly totally alone much of the way to Mexico. They will join with others to roost overnight. The number of close to 50 million is still much smaller than the over a billion in 1997, showing a definite decline in Monarchs coming from different locales.

Imagine this: they will make their grand entrance as a group, sometimes extending as far as 50 miles across. The sky can be darkened for miles as this "band of orange and black" flies as a huge cloud to their pre-programmed and appointed destination southwest. One can hear the sound of their flapping wings that sounds like rain. There could be countless millions of Monarchs who start the journey but many will never finish. **Only a remnant will safely arrive HOME.**

This applies to humans in the same way. We are born and live out our lifetime one day at a time. Throughout our journey, we have opportunities to reach out and accept what Jesus did for each one of us. But God won't impose His will upon anyone. **We are all born with something called "free will" which means WE make the decision to go to Heaven or not.** We will never be forced to choose Heaven, if we say "no". In **Matthew 7:13-14** it says:

"Enter through the narrow gate; for the gate is wide and the way is broad that leads to destruction, and there are many who enter through it. For the gate is small and the way is narrow that leads to life, and there are many who enter through it. How narrow is the gate and difficult the road that leads to life, and few find it."

What this means is the narrow way to get to our ultimate destination of Heaven WILL NOT be travelled by most, **but few**. It's always easier to go the way of the world and follow what they think is "normal" instead of going the way of the Bible which always leads us HOME if we will do what God says. It is our responsibility to find that narrow road and walk on it, no matter what path the world chooses.

We all travel individually – as well as the Monarch butterfly, and if we make the right decision to follow the Lord, we will one day join the company of millions and millions throughout history who have made that all-important decision. Our family members and friends who have accepted Jesus as their Savior will be there. What a day that will be to see them again. It is through the Bible and its wisdom plus the examples of those who have been, are now, or will be in our lives, that show us by their examples in word and deed, that will help guide us to our eternal HOME. In this way, we are showing others how to walk the "narrow path" on our journey on this earth. We must remember that this earth **IS NOT** our final destination – Heaven is our HOME!!

Because we are a spirit that his a mind and lives in a body, **we will NEVER die!** We will go to Heaven as God's child to dwell with Him forever. If we refuse what He has offered us through His Son, Jesus Christ – our final destination will be Hell. **As the late Rev. E.V. Hill used to say: "There ain't no exists there."**

Chapter 13

OVER THE RIVERS AND
THROUGH THOSE WOODS

The Monarch butterfly's wingspan is 4" wide and its weight is less than 1/5 of an ounce or as much as a postage stamp. **How in the world can something the size of a leaf fly across a continent?** They are so fragile and yet they are able to survive this migration by the millions. It has mystical significance and is a phenomenon for sure. (1)

These butterflies are following something that scientists are just beginning to get answers to. When the changes in daylight during the late summer comes it is an indication of the approach of winter. This causes the Monarch butterflies' magnetic molecules to be switched on which helps them to orientate themselves in a south to south-west direction -- something that is absolutely critical to survive. There is no room for error. They know they must leave Canada for the 3000-mile trip ahead.

The amazing fact is that they are freshly hatched **and never flew before**, let alone for any long distance. Only since 1976 have their migratory habits been discovered. There is a biological compass within them that is a pair of molecules in their brains that allows them to sense the direction of the earth's magnetic field that becomes their guide like a compass. They can use this in combination with information from the position of the sun. This occurs on a day in autumn when day and night are the same length.

The strenuous trip begins. Note that these Monarch butterflies fly only in perfect conditions. If it's too hot, their flying stops. If it's too cold, they become sluggish.

Either way, conditions have to be just right. The miraculous part of this is that Monarch butterflies begin the long trip from many many different starting points, yet all arrive in Mexico at the same time. How is that possible? (1)

They have the worst possible body form to make this very dangerous trip. They expend twenty times more the energy than is actually necessary to fly. They make up for that by soaring and gliding on rising currents of air. It is absolutely necessary that they use prevailing winds to get them to their destination on time. If the conditions are good, they can maintain or gain altitude quickly, staying within a stream of rising air. Soaring is the key to getting them **HOME** to Mexico. **Their destination will be a plot of ground that is only sixty miles wide and 10,000 feet high. So they must fly 50 to 100 miles daily so they will end up in the identical place as their grandparents did for generations before them.**

Their speed in flight is around **12 miles per hour.** Many millions of Monarch butterflies travel at least 3000 miles, depending upon where they began their flight from Canada and the upper United States. However, only about one in five survive the trip. But that doesn't matter to them. These Monarch butterflies are determined to get to their destination and nothing will stop them. But they will have to work very hard in order to survive the very long trip.

On this strenuous trip southwest they will encounter many things that they will have to overcome. **The first huge obstacle will be the Great Lakes.** This will be their first geophysical encounter. Ahead of them are miles of water and shifting winds, adding up to a huge barrier. **It's impossible to see across the water because there is no land that is visible for them to get their bearings.** So they will have to use their sense of direction and allow the winds to carry them across the water. They may stop and land on a ship that is passing by them in order to rest or if the winds are blowing in the wrong direction. As soon as they sense the winds have shifted, they will continue on their journey.

Isn't that the same with us humans? We do not have a perfect life for sure.

Problems develop throughout life. Sometimes decisions we have made can get us into trouble. Sickness and disease can occur. Problems in our family can pop up and stay a long time. Disappointments and sadness can come. Things can go wrong that we have no control over. BUT through all of these things in life, when we stay close to the Lord throughout these occurrences, He always makes it turn out right.

We are never to turn away from God. Things happen in our lives that we don't want, or can fully understand, but that doesn't mean that we stop believing in God and that He is doing what only He can do to make our lives meaningful.

The key to surviving all of these disappointments in life is to **keep praising God, no matter what happens.** If we allow Him to be in control of those situations, and if our faith remains intact, and if we have that vital day-by-day relationship with Him, His perfect will shall be accomplished. **His wisdom is far greater and higher than ours and His decisions override ours.** Remain connected to Him and He will protect, guide, lead, and bless your life. **Proverbs 3:5-6** says it very well: **"Trust in the Lord with all your heart, and do not rely on your own understanding; in all your ways acknowledge Him, and He will make your paths straight." John 16:33** says: **"I have told you these things so that in Me you may have peace. You will have suffering in this world. Be courageous! I have conquered the world."**

Chapter 14

THE ENEMY NEVER GIVES UP

The hurdles in front of these Monarch butterflies on their trip south are never ending. There are spiders, wasps, ants, frogs, and even ladybugs. A hungry cat can even pose a threat. Whether it's the beginning of their trip, midway, or even after they have finally arrived at their destination, the enemy never gives up. As millions and millions hover together on the trees in Mexico, there are still predators lurking. They include Black Headed Orioles and Black Backed Grosbeaks who enjoy attacking these hibernating insects. On the ground we find Black Eared Mice gobbling up those Monarch butterflies who have fallen from the trees. **What are these enemies after? Fat. A colony of 50 million**

Monarch butterflies has as much fat as 1500 pounds of butter! (1)

As believers in Jesus, it is an absolute necessity that we be on guard at all times, lest the sly attacker, called the devil – places snares and traps ahead of us to cause us to fall spiritually away from God. We must know his tactics in order to be one step ahead of him. This only comes from a thorough knowledge of the Bible and a day-to-day relationship with God. We, too, are on our journey HOME, and the enemy will do everything he can to stop us from our designated journey's destination.

The Monarch butterflies, during this fall migration, must accumulate enough energy for the long flight ahead, as well as the five months' wintering period, and even extending into the spring northward flight – if there are very few flowers available they can land on. How do these butterflies last this long without little water or nectar? It is an absolute mystery.

Christians are told by the Lord in **I Peter 5:8** to **"Be of sober spirit, be on the alert. Your adversary, the devil, prowls around like a roaring lion, seeking someone to devour."**

But Jesus is called the Lion from God Who is looking out for us. The devil goes around consistently prowling AS a lion, but he really isn't one. He is all mouth and of little substance. We cannot be made afraid by his words in our ears. Why? because the Greater One named Jesus lives on the inside of us as believers, and we are fully capable of overcoming him. But we must be constantly on high alert, no matter where we go in a given day.

Another enemy of the Monarch butterfly is bad weather. As a matter of fact, it can be a very deadly thing. Why? **It's because the Monarch butterfly will die if it gets too wet.**

Then there are also natural obstacles: parasites, disease, viruses and bacteria. It is hard to believe that even though all of these hindrances are there, that millions make it safely to their destination, although far, far fewer than the numbers that began the trip. (2)

As a matter of fact, the same thing applies to us as human beings. We too can be influenced greatly by outside and inside assaults: these being bad attitudes, unforgiveness, poor choices, ungodly influences, harsh words, ill treatment, sickness and disease. These can take a heavy toll and draw us away from the true and living God. But with an eternal **HOME** perspective in our spirit, we will not be as readily influenced by our present circumstances which are subject to change at any given moment. We are told to trust in the Lord with all our hearts no matter what happens that would pull us away from Him and the fulfillment of our divine destiny. **We cannot afford to stop believing in the goodness of God and His sovereignty over our life, no matter what the circumstances are.** It is absolutely necessary that we let God be King over our lives.

Chapter 15

No Straying from the Path

These Monarch butterflies must follow a very specific path. There can be absolutely no room for error. **If they would drift from that precise path, the entire species would become extinct; it's that critical.** The Lord created this wondrous creature and its finely tuned journey to Mexico year after year that has to be followed precisely for their survival.

They have now traveled six weeks from Canada. But the most treacherous part of this trip is over desert and a mountain range that is 900 miles long. These butterflies do not cross over the Gulf of Mexico but travel only by land, not as they did at the beginning of their trip when they flew over the Great Lakes. This leaf-sized insect at this point flies across a continent. And it still remains a beautiful mystery of nature.

How does it know the way? Who has given it such explicit instructions? How can it fly over that long mountain range? How does something as light in weight as a postage stamp withstand the wind that must be blowing hard at times through those mountains? And what about the intense heat? It has been given precise directions from its Creator. It knows, it just knows how to pull it off -without a map. It's that simple without further explanation. (1)

As humans we must follow that perfect path to Heaven because there is only **ONE WAY** to get there. We dare not wander from it. It would lead to our destruction.

It is also an absolute necessity to be in a place of worship where the Minister teaches the whole truth contained within the pages of the Bible. There are Pastors who are disguised as "angels of light" who fill pulpits and have no clue as to what the Bible has to say about the necessity of salvation nor how to get to our eternal destination. These people are sometimes put there because the devil has placed that person in leadership who preaches the wrong things, particularly that you have to be good enough to get to Heaven by your own efforts. That **IS NOT** true. What **IS TRUE** is knowing **Ephesians 2:8-10 "For you are saved by grace through faith, and this is not from works, so that no one can boast."** As a believer, it is absolutely necessary that we know the Bible for ourselves so we an have an edge on what is being spoken from the pulpit. Read scripture daily. If what is spoken from the pulpit doesn't agree with what the Bible proclaims as absolute truth, don't believe it. **II Corinthians 11:13-15** says: **"For such men are false apostles, deceitful workers, disguising themselves as apostles of Christ."** No wonder, for even Satan disguises himself as an angel of light. Therefore, it is not surprising if his servants also disguise themselves as servants of righteousness, whose end will be according to their deeds. The best solution is to read the Bible through from Genesis to Revelation in one year. That way you will get the whole picture that God is unveiling book after book. It all connects together as one story. There is only one path to heaven through the shed blood of Jesus, as pointed out in the Bible. We cannot get there by another way. Stay on course or you will **NEVER get there.**

Where you spend eternity depends on it!

There is only One Way and it's through Jesus. **John 14:6** says **"Jesus said to him, "I am the way, and the truth, and the life; no one comes to the Father but through Me."** If a minister tries to convince you that there is Plan B, reject it.

Matthew 7:13-14 Jesus is speaking: **"Enter through the narrow gate; for the gate is wide and the way is broad that leads to destruction, and there are many who enter through it. For the gate is small and the way is narrow that leads to life, and there are few who find it."** Please note the word **FEW.**

II Timothy 3:16-17 very clearly states: **"All scripture is inspired by God and is profitable for teaching, for rebuking, for correcting, for training in righteousness, so that the man of God may be complete."** It's as if God were standing in front of us personally speaking to us.

In the midst of all that is taking place on this earth, the Word of God must be preached, not only from pulpits, but also from the lips of every

Christian. Because **Habakkuk 2:14** very plainly says: **"For the earth will be filled with the knowledge of the Lord's glory, as the water covers the sea."** That's through our mouths as born-again believers as well as those called to be Pastors.

We are to let the world know that Jesus lives inside us by the way we talk and walk among them. We can't let the world shape us into their thinking. We must be an example of a follower of Jesus Christ to them.

Chapter 16

THEY'RE HERE

In Myahaova, Mexico, many people await the glorious arrival of the Monarch butterflies. This grand entrance causes the Mexicans to celebrate **"The Day of the Dead"** on November 1 and 2. This is the belief that the souls of their departed ones come to them each year on the wings of these butterflies. They also have Catholic services, celebrating the lives of their relatives who loved Jesus Christ in their lifetime. As Nicole Chanez of CNN said on 11/1/19 "It has everything to do with the afterlife, love and those colorful skulls you've seen around" (the area in Mexico where this event occurs). (1)

Mexican children, men and women, young and old, as well as tourists from around the world, are anxiously awaiting for the Monarch butterflies' arrival, because of the beauty of these creatures and their awesome numbers.

They are all straining their eyes as their heads turn this way and that. But the sky seems to be empty. Nothing. But wait......suddenly they see a few of these beautiful orange, black and white beauties. Then more. Then the sky becomes darkened with millions and millions of them.

These living mosaics that look like a whole cathedral in flight enter the skies around their final destination. Shouting and crying, singing and clapping is heard everywhere. **"They've come back" is their unified cry.** The celebration begins. Cameras begin to click and videos begin to roll. Cell phones with cameras are recording this glorious event. Let the party begin! Fireworks are shot into the air, color, noise, people, the smell of food, vendors chanting their wares, all relating to the Monarch butterflies. And most of all, the butterflies have covered every inch of sky and ground around them. What a mix! (Going to this website will give you pictures of this event.) (2)

These Mexicans must rely on the money they receive from the tourists from around the world during this special envelope of time, in order to make a living for the rest of the year. That's quite an under- taking, but they succeed year after year.

male

The Monarch but- terflies return to only twelve specific conifer pine tree groves. They fly immediately to the limbs and trunks of the huge trees and they hang on for dear life – sometimes even to the same trees their ancestors did in times past. When

Female

they fly in these enormous numbers of millions and millions, they sound like loud falling rain. **Often a huge branch they are clinging to will break from the sheer weight of these butterflies, since it is capable of holding as many as 15,000 at a time.** As little as 15 years ago there were one billion of them but now the numbers have been considerably reduced to millions. (3)

Even the water supplies for Monarchs after hibernation are drying up as well, which are critical to their survival.

These tree branches serve as a huge umbrella that shields these butterflies from the rain, which can be very deadly. The hot sun's rays are also shielded from these butterflies by the canopy of tree branches. As the Monarch butterflies huddle together on the tree trunks and branches, they are able to keep their heat inside them. Since the high mountains of Mexico are located in the clouds, this also provides the right amount of moisture as they hibernate. These oyamel fir trees are so called for the Christian cross at the branch tips.

If the temperature dips below freezing however, this could prove to be as deadly as if they got wet. They are now clinging to the tree trunks and branches for survival. Frost will kill them if they drop to the forest floor. Remember, they only weigh 1/5 of a penny. 80% of them could die at once. They are an endangered miracle.

One would think these Monarch butterflies are now safe. They have traveled for 3000 miles and now they can rest. Not so. There is another huge obstacle and great danger to their migratory plan.

The selected forests where they spend the winter have been victims of stripping by illegal loggers. These huge oyamel fir forests in the Sierra Madrae Mountains are being cut down to dangerously low numbers. In 1986 the Mexican government protected the butterflies, and these trees were totally off limits to loggers. Improvement is essential. It has always seemed the right thing to do for the survival of these Mexican families. Dr. Bill Calvert has noted that in reality the Monarch's future generations have been at risk. Then according to AP News Mexico City in 2013, this illegal logging has almost been stopped, which is excellent news. (4)

There are fewer huge trees left that the Monarchs could very easily freeze to death if they try to find shelter in the remaining small trees, simply because they provide so little protection from the elements. Then if they get too wet or too cold from unusually cold winters this could prove to be a disaster. 80% of them could die at once. Monarch butterflies are an endangered phenomena. If the huge trees are cut down, this yearly migration would totally disappear from the earth.

The Monarch butterflies hibernate from December to March and eat very little but survive on the fat stored in their bodies. Now and then they will drink a little water from a nearby stream or sip a little nectar from nearby flowers if any are nearby.

But for five months they hang tightly together in hibernation. According to Dr. Karen Oberhauser of Journey North, Monarch butterflies are cold blooded. So snow and ice crystals can kill them. 80-90% can die if they even become wet. Temperature and survival are a delicate balance tween warm and cold at this point.

When this hibernation is completed they will fly down from these huge trees and will sit in the mud from which they get nutrients and minerals. They will only become airborne when the weather is much warmer.

As spring approaches, it is mandatory that they go north and east. It is absolutely essential that they mate and begin stage one of a new generation all over again. By next winter, another distinct generation will return to this same place that these ancestors left the year before.

Monarch butterflies obtain sugar that is converted into lipids as their energy source. They will get nectar from fields of clover and goldenrod and other nectar- producing flowers on their migratory trip back north to Canada.

Because Monarch butterflies can be found across the world, they will never totally become extinct. They can survive in warm climates on a year-round basis, but northern U.S. and Canada where the winters are bitter, that is impossible.

Even the much smaller route west of the Rockies is producing smaller numbers as they fly to California to hibernate there in the warm winters of the state.

Because the large masses of Monarch butterflies migrated southwest to the forest reserve in Mexico that covers 193,000 acres, some scientists believe that there is a possibility that the butterflies have released chemicals that in some way "show the way" on their designated path to their destination in Mexico. However, as the numbers decrease on a continual basis and the numbers reach an unbelievably low level, there could be such little chemical traces that the butterflies would not be able to find their way HOME.

A second-generation guide named Emilio Valezquez Moreno who has been a vital part of the Monarch migration extending back to his childhood, made the statement, "We have to protect this. This comes first, this is our heritage."

Chapter 17

THE CYCLE REPEATS ITSELF

I t's Spring Equinox (when day and night are of equal length across this earth), and that may cause the Monarch butterflies to begin their flight back north. They open their wings to the warming of the sun on them. Dr. Bill Calvert, one of the first biologists to study Monarch butterflies, has spent the most time with them. He wrote of this awakening from hibernation, quote: "Flying in a frenzy, a golden flow, an explosion of orange, a blizzard of butterflies – flapping, gliding, mating, drinking – so many Monarchs we could hardly breathe." (1)

They take off for northern Texas during the second and third week of March.

They are beginning the 3000 mile trip back north to Canada where come fall and the migration south will happen all over again. The conservation of nectar plants in Texas and northern Mexico is very critical to sustaining the Monarch butterflies' migration. Most of these Monarch butterflies will first fly to Texas, then fly back north in masses. On the way, they will mate. The females again will lay many fertilized eggs on milkweed plants along the way, laying one egg at a time. **Then these parents will die (the ones that hibernated all winter) – because their purpose is complete.**

Their species will continue. When the new generation hatches, they will fly further north while mating along the way. It will be a year before the process is repeated and they return to Mexico. They will reach Canada again and die. But before they do they will give birth to the first generation that will live one and a half months. The second and third generations live only weeks also but the fourth generation will live over seven months, longer than the other generations. The cycle continues, and they will turn around and fly south.

It has been almost a full year since the migration began. The fourth generation will be born in

Canada and the miraculous migration will begin once again.

When Monarchs butterflies arrive in the northern part of the United States early in the Spring, they may be able to squeeze in an extra generation in some areas.

This is only possible where Monarch butterflies arrived early or the temperatures are unusually warm.

This migration is part of our American culture. The Monarch butterflies are some of the most magnificent insects in the whole world. Year after year their migration to Mexico is amazing to everyone who learns about it for the first time, and every time after that. **They certainly have flown on a very incredible journey HOME. There is nothing that can compare with it in the whole insect kingdom.**

Acclaimed Mexican poet, novelist, environmentalist, journalist, and diplomat Homero Aridjis, known for his rich imagination, poetry of lyrical beauty, and ethical independence, has written a poem entitled:

TO A MONARCH BUTTERFLY

**You who go through the sky
Like a winged tiger
Burning as you fly
Tell me what supernatural life
Is painted on your wings
So that after this life
I may see you in my night**

(Translated by George McWhirter) (2)

These Monarch butterflies have an unquench-able drive to go HOME, even though they have no maps or GPS. **Instead their navigation system is inside their bodies.** And they make it there every year without fail at the exact same time. This will continue for generations to come, as long as there is enough milkweed, nectar producing plants, temperature levels in Mexico that will not cause them to freeze during their hibernation period, and that the huge pine trees where they hang on for five months remains intact and are not cut down.

How mysterious is the correlation between the Monarch butterfly and the born-again Christian on our way to our final **HOME.** However, the undisputed difference between us is this: **Monarch butterflies continue to struggle once they have arrived at their designated HOME in Mexico. But those who have accepted Jesus Christ as personal Savior in their lifetime, have FULL ASSURANCE that they will arrive safely once that decision has been made and as a result will spend eternity in peace with the Lord Jesus Christ.**

Chapter 18

BORN TO FLY

B efore bringing this book to a conclusion, it is
my pleasure to share three of the occasions in
my lifetime that I have had a personal and upfront
encounter with Monarch butterflies:

On one occasion it was the Fall season and I
spied a beautiful Monarch perched on a light pink
annual impatien flower in our back yard. The day
was very cool because Fall was nearing an end. The
butterfly didn't move from the flower's petals as I
moved up close. I admired it and then walked away.
I didn't think of it again until late evening when
I was getting ready to go to bed. Thoughts of the
Monarch butterfly did return to me. I wondered if
it were still out there on the impatien.

Just in case it was, I gathered up a small cardboard box in which I had placed a soft cloth inside. I put on a coat because the temperature had dropped even more. I found a flashlight in the kitchen drawer and went out through the garage, down the hill to the impatien bed of flowers where I had seen it hours before. I shined the flashlight where I had seen it and there it sat. The temperature was only in the 40's so it was "stuck" so to speak. I gathered it up and placed it into the box and brought it into the house. I put it in the dining room on a stand and went to bed. The next morning I dashed downstairs to the dining room where I had left the Monarch butterfly the night before. It wasn't in the box. I looked around and there it was, sitting on the brass chandelier hanging over the dining room table. I was puzzled as to how to capture it in order to release it back to the outside. The temperature had gone up and the sun was shining. At this point, the Monarch butterfly would be able to withstand the elements. I walked up to it, and it stepped onto my extended hand without hesitation. It had used our home for a chance to warm up and rest before continuing on its way the next morning. So I took it to the front door which I opened and away it flew. What a memorable experience.

Another Monarch visitation was a Divine set up as well. Our family found a Monarch butterfly in a parking lot of a General Store as we were exploring Amish Country in Ohio where we live. It was just sitting there on the gravel in the lot. Apparently it had crashed into the windshield of a car on its way to a flower. I picked it up and laid it on the floor of our car. After our day of touring the area we drove home. I placed it into a small cardboard box with a cloth inside (I guess this is what I always bring out when I see a Monarch butterfly who needs help). I placed a small container of diluted honey alongside the butterfly not knowing if it would partake or not. It was in our home for about two weeks. It did drink the honey water. I would perch it on my finger or I would carry it around on a small pillow where it rode along where I went. It didn't attempt to fly so it was fun to have it with me.

The day came when I decided it had recuperated to the point that it was time to "launch" it into nature again so it could fly away.

Our daughter, Diahann, was a teenager and was enthralled by our little butterfly friend. I carried the box outside as we walked to the front yard. I gave her the box and she put the Monarch butterfly on her forefinger. She dipped her arm down low to the grass and then back up very quickly. The Monarch butterfly was hanging on for dear life. It finally did let go but only flew about 20 feet. We did that routine a few more times. But it was evident that it wasn't going anywhere. So we took it back inside the house and in a few more days Diahann and I repeated the same procedure. It had finally figured out what to do and flew away around the south side of our home, never to be seen again. This was such a small creature that God had made, but He allowed a human being to nurse it back to a state of health enabling it to fly away, as was intended.

One day during the next Spring season Diahann came running into the kitchen. "Mom, you've got to come to the back yard and see something beautiful." We ran outside and down to the bottom of the hill where there was a bush honeysuckle in bloom. There sitting on the branches was one Monarch butterfly after another. It looked like the bush was blooming living orange and gold flowers. Apparently, God had sidetracked this traveling group of Monarch butterflies right to our yard. Our area in Ohio was not on any migratory path of Monarch butterflies. But God was saying to us in essence, "Thanks for caring for one of my small Monarch butterflies. Here's a whole bush of them to enjoy." That was remarkable!

The most memorable occasion encountering a Monarch butterfly occurred on Labor Day 2012. My daughter, Diahann, her husband, John and family were at our home for a picnic. We were in the backyard that is full of flower gardens. Our ten year old granddaughter, Claire, saw a Monarch butterfly caterpillar sitting on a milkweed leaf of one of the numerous plants there. She shouted out that there was another caterpillar, then another. We counted 12!! We decided to take them all inside and make sure they were able to develop into the Monarch butterflies they were to be without incident. I gave six of them to our three grandchildren (including Cate and Chris). My husband, Bob and I kept 6.

They all advanced from the caterpillar state to the adult Monarch butterfly with no problem – except for one of ours and one of theirs. Our Monarch butterflies came forth as adults. In one day, two emerged that I had which were a male and a female. By late afternoon they were both successfully launched. Up, Up and away they flew. Now airborne, they began the long, long trip to Mexico.

The next day, two more females came out of their chrysalises. By late afternoon these two flew off to finally join the other Monarch butterflies from other states on their way south.

Last of all, a female Monarch butterfly who will be in my memory forever, came out of her chrysalis. She was born at 7:30 a.m. I was planning on launching her that day, although it was very cloudy, and once in a while there was a slight drizzle. The sun peeked out at noon. I took the newly born butterfly out to the patio and reached into the little screened cage and removed it from its temporary quarters. She sat on my right forefinger for half an hour without moving her body. But her little black head went back and forth and in essence said, "No, I am not leaving you". I would keep telling it to "fly away to Mexico. You have a very long trip to make". A Monarch butterfly's flight muscles must be warm enough to fly. If it's a cloudy day and the temperature is not 55 degrees or above, they won't budge.

That little creation from God wanted to stay with me. The rain had started to sprinkle again and I didn't want to launch her into a rain-filled atmosphere. So I put her back into the cage without any resistance from her.

That day I took her everywhere I went in our home. She was content to remain in the cage. I would talk to her and told her I appreciated her being a part of my life for such a few days, and that she brought me a lot of joy.

As morning arrived, I woke up at 5:00 am so I could arrive at our daughter's home by 7:15, in order to take care of our four-year-old granddaughter, Cate. We would spend the morning together before I gave her lunch. Then she would dress, and I would take her to pre-school. As I arrived at Diahann's home, I told Cate that we would launch the Monarch butterfly from the cage after the temperature outside was above 55 degrees and the sun was shining.

It was now 9:30 am, and the sun had caused the temperature to rise. The fog was gone, and it was delightfully warm as I opened the back door to check. So Cate and I went out the door and down the steps, with the cage in my right hand and the Monarch butterfly inside. I opened the little door on the front of the cage. She was flopping around and ready to take flight. Out she came, and up she went into the beautiful blue sky. "Goodbye my dear friend", I said. "Thank you for coming into our life for too short a time. I will never forget you." Cate and I went back into their home to play games before lunch and a morning in pre-school.

At 10:30 or so we went upstairs to her bedroom, in order for her to change from p.j.'s to school clothes. After helping her get dressed, we came out of her bedroom and started down the steps to the landing. There are 24 windows in Diahann and John's home. At the landing, there was a honeycomb blind covering the window. I noticed a small shadow near the bottom of the pulled-down blind. Thinking it was probably a grasshopper, I pulled back the blind. There sat the beautiful Monarch butterfly that I had just launched over an hour before. I thought she was long gone by now. But somehow she knew I would be at that specific window at that time of day. I touched the glass where she was, and she flew up and out of sight. We had some kind of connection between a human and a butterfly.

Romans 1:20 says so plainly: "**For His invisible attributes, that is, His eternal power and divine nature, have been clearly seen since the creation of the world, being understood through what He has made. As a result, people are without excuse.**"

This beautiful magnificent insect called the Monarch butterfly had, for one moment, been made to "communicate" with a human. Both the butterfly and I were created by the same loving hands of God to fly away to our final **HOME** at the end of life's journey here, where we will be united with those who have shown us the way for centuries.

This Monarch butterfly phenomenon is a vivid example of the faithfulness of God. The tides go in and out on a daily basis on the shores of the ocean, the sun rises and sets faithfully day after day, the seasons have remained since God put them in place, the daffodils inside lifeless dry bulbs know exactly which month to come forth as a delightful fragrant flower, and the Canadian geese know instinctively how to fly in a V formation, without any flight instructor. How can we fathom the mind of Almighty God who put into this Monarch butterfly, the wisdom to show us humans our way **HOME?**

To the reader of this book: "Please come and join my family and me. When the perfect time comes, we will all fly singly to our eternal **HOME, but we will all meet at the same destination, if we have accepted Jesus as our Savior in our lifetime.**

I Thessalonians 4:14-18 says: **"For if we believe that Jesus died and rose again, in the same way, through Jesus, God will bring with Him those who have fallen asleep. For we say to you by a word from the Lord: We who are still alive at the Lord's coming, we will certainly not precede those who have fallen asleep. For the Lord Himself will descend from Heaven with a shout, with the archangel's voice, and with a trumpet of God, and the dead in Christ will rise first. Then we who are still alive, who are left, will be caught up together with them in the clouds to meet the Lord in the air, and so we will always be with the Lord. Therefore encourage one another with these words."**

If we have not passed from this earth in a natural death – and the Lord Jesus comes in our lifetime, we will meet Him in the air and travel to our **ETERNAL HOME**.

Chapter 19

OBEDIENCE/DISOBEDIENCE = FINAL DESTINATION

In 2019 I raised five Monarch butterflies, and one of which was lost.

With four of them, everything went as planned. However, with the fifth one, there was a resistance to "The Plan of God".

This caterpillar would eat some of the milkweed leaves (which was its pathway to developing into the chrysalis state). But for hours it would just lie on a milkweed leaf without proceeding any further. It didn't feel like moving forward and eating.

This went on for days. Programmed inside the caterpillar is the progression from that stage to its final stage as a caterpillar, as it attaches itself to something higher than it's ever been. It has to let go and trust that what it's attached to will hold it secure, as it moves into the J form for 24 hours. It then disappears into the chrysalis, which is 1/3 the size of the grown caterpillar. In 10-14 days, the beautiful butterfly emerges and flies away.

But this fifth caterpillar in captivity would eat and sleep, eat and sleep. That's it! Finally, it decided it was done with eating and looked for a "landing place". It tried the small branch that was propped up inside the cage. But no – that wasn't good enough. It hung on the screen of the cage sideways for hours. Finally, it decided to attach according to "The Plan of God". It did attach and dropped down. The J form appeared. I thought by morning it would be transformed into the chrysalis.

When the morning light came and I opened the blind in front of it, I saw the chrysalis on the bottom of the cage. What was hanging was a very narrow version of the head and body of the butterfly that was to have developed. It was now impossible because the safety of the chrysalis was gone, and it had slipped from the position of being "kept" securely.

I had to bury what was left. I put on vinyl gloves and pulled the stiff body from the top of the cage.

As I began picking up the chrysalis it broke open, and a liquid of black, orange, yellow-gold and white oozed out. This was the DNA of every part of the Monarch that was to have developed. The remains were put into a plastic bag and buried.

Because of the laziness and disobedience of that caterpillar, it missed the glory of its destiny ahead to become a beautiful Monarch butterfly, had it only obeyed.

What a vivid example for us as humans.

We are born with the desire to "do it my way", but then realize what we are doing isn't working. And so we must accept Jesus Christ as the One Who paid the ultimate price for our rebellion. And as long as we confess our sins, ask for forgiveness, accept Him into our life, have a relationship with Him, read our Bible regularly and live a life that is pleasing to God, we will go to heaven at the end of our lives.

But we still live here with our free will. **Our choices do determine our destiny.**

We either hang on tightly to the hand of God – no matter what the problem, disappointment, ridicule or unbelief of those around us – or we give in and continue to rebel, and finally end up in a place

God never intended, which is Hell. Our destiny of Heaven is forever gone. **There is no second chance after we die.**

A perfect example of this concerns one of the hand-picked twelve disciples of Jesus. Eleven of them died, not turning their backs on Jesus in their lifetimes. Ten died deaths that we cannot fully grasp. The one remaining who was John, died as a very old man, but still went through some very terrible circumstances before his death. Yet all eleven kept believing in Heaven as their final **HOME** after this earth.

Judas was one of those special men whom Jesus chose to work by His side, learning and doing what He did for 3-1/2 years of ministry. All twelve were His students, so to speak, learning and working daily with the Master, to restore those who were ill and lost without God in their lives.

MATTHEW 10:8 declares: **"Heal the sick, raise the dead, cleanse those with leprosy. Drive out demons. Freely you received, freely give."** Jesus' instructions were profound, even extending to the raising the dead to life again.

John 15:7 says: **"If you remain in Me and My words remain in you, ask whatever you want and**

it will be done for you. My Father is glorified by this: that you produce much fruit and prove to be My disciples."

But the day came when Judas didn't want to cling to his teacher, guide, Savior and Lord anymore. He rebelled and wanted to do things "his way" instead.

Before Jesus went to the cross to die for the sins of every human that has ever lived or ever will live, He participated in a supper called the Passover, the sacred meal of the Jews which occurs every year in the Spring. This same occurrence Christians call The Last Supper, in which Jesus had His disciples participate with Him in taking the bread and wine as symbols of His broken body and shed blood.

As Jesus ate with His 12 disciples, He called out the rebellious disciple without even mentioning His name – only what he was about to do: **Matthew 26:23** says: **He replied, "The one who dipped his hand with Me in the bowl, he will betray Me." Verse 25: Judas, His betrayer replied, "Surely not I, Rabbi." "You have said it"** Jesus told him. Judas declared his guilt out of his own mouth.

This disciple who, at the beginning, had loved Jesus dearly – turned his back on the Only One who was willing to pay the ultimate price to get him **HOME** to Heaven by forgiving all of Judas' sins.

Judas went to the religious leaders of the day and said he would show them Who this person was who they wanted to destroy (for a price). The people were following after Jesus and turning from the religious leaders. He was going about healing the sick, and even raising the dead. That infuriated the Pharisees. They agreed to give this betrayer 30 pieces of silver to point Him out to them so they could do away with Him once and for all. Judas then took those leaders to the place where Jesus prayed frequently. He pointed Him out, and they grabbed the Only One Who could have gotten Judas into Heaven, as well as the ones who wanted to do away with the Savior of the world.

When this horrible plan of the disobedient disciple of Jesus was finally realized, instead of going to Jesus and getting in front of Him to plead for His forgiveness, Judas went to the wrong people – the religious leaders. In **Matthew 27:4** it says: **"I have sinned by betraying innocent blood",** Judas cried out. They didn't care one bit. In **Verse 5** it says **"so he threw the silver into the temple and departed. Then he went and hanged himself."**

His Only Way to God was gone! He didn't have any more chances. Because of disobedience, he forfeited his way to God in his life, not asking for forgiveness from the only One who could. It is written: **Hebrews 9:27a "and just as it is appointed for people to die once-and after this, judgment"** we see plainly that death is an appointed time by God Himself. But after we pass from this earth, there is no way to come to Jesus as Savior. We have either made that decision during our lifetime or we totally missed it! Forever!

And this applies to us. We have the opportunity to accept the Jesus into our lives.

If we say no, then we will have sealed our own destiny to Hell by our wrong decision.

Cate and I have made that commitment to follow Jesus all the days of our lives.

She is 14 and I am 83. She made that commitment at 4, and I did at 36.

Ralph Waldo Emerson once wrote: "Do not go where the path may lead. Go instead where there is no path and leave a trail."

Cate and I know that we will go to heaven. **We will be waiting for you. Don't miss it for anything!**

NOTES

1 – LAYING THE FOUNDATION

World Challenge Pulpit Series by David Wilkerson (Under "The Costliness of Possessing Christ" www.worldchallenge.org

1. Wikipedia W (11) Wanderer Butterfly, Australian Museum, nature culture – Discoverer, Sidney, Australia, Retrieved 2010

2 – CIRCULAR BEGINNINGS

1. Urquhart, F, 1987. The Monarch Butterfly: International Traveler. Nelson Hall

2. W(16) Oberhauser, Karen S.; Michelle J. Solensky (2004) The Monarch Butterfly; Biology and Conservation, Cornell University Press pp.3 (W17) Monarch Life Cycle, Biology, Monarch Watch – Both Wickipedia

3. www.webrmd.com/baby/ss/slideshow. conception

3 – CHOMP, CHOMP, DUMP, DUMP

1. WikipediaW(19) James A. Scott (1986) The Butterflies of North America, Stanford

4 – ALWAYS BEING WATCHED

None

5 – MANY BLACK SHOES

1. Same as Chapter 3 – 1.

2. www.activewild.com

6 – THE SACRIFICE OF LAMBS

None

7 – IT'S A TRANSFORMATION

1. ourhabitatgarden.org

8 – HANG ON TIGHT

1. Lincoln P. Brower, Sweet Briar College: http://biology.sbc.edu/Research/Mex_ NSF/PROJECT_ Absgtrat.htm

2. www.biologysbc.edu/faculty/ BrowerpublishJan2010.htm

9 – GOD'S GLORY DOTS

1. Askentomologists.com

2. www.webmd.com/baby/ss/slideshow. conception

10 – THE SINNER'S PRAYER

None

11 – A MIRACLE HAPPENS

1. City Folk nookipedia.com/wiki/ Monarch-butterfly

2. Monarchbutterflyusa.com/scale-wing

12 – ONE, TWO, THREE, FOUR

1. milliontrees.me.2013/11/0l. monarchbutterflies

2. Wikipedia (W) 20 Pyle, Robert Michael, "National Audubon Society Field Guide to North American Butterflies" Pgs 712-713

3. Wickipedia Ramiarez, Maria Isabel; Azarate, Joaquin G.,Luna, Laura (April 2002) "Effects of human activities on Monarch Butterfly habitat in protected mountain forests, Mexico." Forestry Chronicle "Canadian Institute of Forestry" 79(2)242-246

13 – OVER THE RIVERS AND THROUGH THOSE WOODS

1. Urquhart, F 1987. The Monarch Butterfly: International Traveler. Nelson Hall

14 – THE ENEMY NEVER GIVES UP

1. Journeynorth.org – Monarch

2. Wickipedia (W)52 John E. Losey, Linda S. Raylor and Maureen E. Carter (1999). "Transgenic pollen harms Monarch larvae. Pdf Nature 399 (6713):214

15 – NO STRAYING FROM THE PATH

1. www.mexperience.com

16 – THEY'RE HERE

1. Journeynorth.org

2. Shutterstock.com picture 1214922625

3. www.learner.org/jnorth/tm/monarch/
   CalvertBio.html Dr. Calvert was one of
   the first biologists to study the Monarchs
   at their over-wintering sites in Mexico, and
   was certainly the one who spent the most
   time with the butterflies, along with Dr.
   Lincoln Brower. Quote from Dr. Brower:
   "Why should we care? For the same reasons we care about the Mona Lisa or the
   beauty of Mozart's music."

4. AP News Mexico City

17 – THE CYCLE REPEATS ITSELF

1. www.learner.org/jnorth/monarch/
   index.html

2. Homero Aridjis en.wikipedia.or/wiki/
   Homero-Arid

18 – NONE

19 – NONE

REFERENCES

The following are three websites to investigate lots of information about three men who had a great deal to do with discovering these Monarch butterflies, and then as they traveled to Mexico on a yearly basis.

Lincoln P. Brower – Sweetwater College (his background and what he accomplished in regard to the Monarch butterflies from 1931-2018).

Dr. Fred A. Urquhart (1911-2002) – a Canadian scientist. The first person to tag Monarch butterflies as they went on their journey to Mexico, as well as their migration year after year.

WWW.LEARNER.ORG/NORTH/TM/
MONARCH/CALVERTBIO.HTML

The third man listed named Dr. Bill Calvert, a Biologist, has studied Monarch butterflies for years. He was obsessed with these butterflies from childhood and who has devoted his life to revealing the mysteries of the Monarch butterflies.

In addition, below are websites to give you further information about Monarch butterflies: Journeynorth.org January 20, 2021

Monarch Joint Venture. Information about the current numbers of Monarchs on trees in Mexico. Also included are: Read the Monarch Action List

Read about how to get involved

<u>WWW.LEARNABOUTNATURE.COM</u> – The story of the Monarch butterflies and how to raise them.

WICKIPEDIA MONARCH BUTTERFLY – Additional facts about them.

NOVA MONARCH BUTTERFLY
THIS IS A PBS FILM TITLED "THE
INCREDIBLE JOURNEY OF THE
BUTTERFLIES" WHICH IS VERY
EXCITING TO WATCH, AS THE
MONARCH BUTTERFLY FLIES ON ITS
3500 MILE JOURNEY TO MEXICO.
PUBLIC BROADCASTING SERVICE, 2100
CRYSTAL DR., ARLINGTON, VA. 22202

MONARCHS ON TREES IN MEXICO
Breathtaking images of the millions of Monarch
butterflies hibernating on the trees all winter
in Mexico.

Interestinginsects.com (Kits to raise them
over winter.)

CPSIA information can be obtained
at www.ICGtesting.com
Printed in the USA
JSHW041929060721
16617JS00003B/18

9 781662 814297